THE GREAT FIRES

JACK GILBERT
THE GREAT FIRES

POEMS 1982 – 1992

ALFRED A. KNOPF   NEW YORK   2005

THIS IS A BORZOI BOOK
PUBLISHED BY ALFRED A. KNOPF, INC.

COPYRIGHT © 1994 BY JACK GILBERT

ALL RIGHTS RESERVED UNDER INTERNATIONAL AND PAN-AMERICAN
COPYRIGHT CONVENTIONS. PUBLISHED IN THE UNITED STATES BY
ALFRED A. KNOPF, INC., NEW YORK, AND SIMULTANEOUSLY IN CANADA
BY RANDOM HOUSE OF CANADA LIMITED, TORONTO. DISTRIBUTED
BY RANDOM HOUSE, INC., NEW YORK.

OWING TO LIMITATIONS OF SPACE, ACKNOWLEDGMENTS FOR PERMIS-
SION TO REPRINT PREVIOUSLY PUBLISHED MATERIAL MAY BE FOUND
FOLLOWING PAGE 90.

LIBRARY OF CONGRESS CATALOGING-IN-PUBLICATION DATA

GILBERT, JACK.
THE GREAT FIRES : POEMS 1982–1992 / BY JACK GILBERT. — 1ST ED.
P.   CM.
ISBN 0-679-42576-4   ISBN 0-679-74767-2 (PBK.)
I. TITLE.
PS3557.I34217G7   1994
811'.54—DC20   93-5701
CIP

MANUFACTURED IN THE UNITED STATES OF AMERICA
PUBLISHED MARCH 20, 1995
REPRINTED SIX TIMES
EIGHTH PRINTING, JUNE 2005

FOR

Michiko Nogami

KAKUBAKARI   KOISHIKUSHI   ARABA
MASOKAGAMI   MINU   HI   TOKI   NAKU
ARAMASHIMONOWO

Manyoshu 4221

*My thanks to the Robert Francis Trust
for an appointment to a poetry residency
at Fort Juniper during the two years when
certain of these poems were written.*

THE GREAT FIRES

The fish are dreadful. They are brought up
the mountain in the dawn most days, beautiful
and alien and cold from night under the sea,
the grand rooms fading from their flat eyes.
Soft machinery of the dark, the man thinks,
washing them. "What can you know of my machinery!"
demands the Lord. *Sure,* the man says quietly
and cuts into them, laying back the dozen struts,
getting to the muck of something terrible.
The Lord insists: "You are the one who chooses
to live this way. I build cities where things
are human. I make Tuscany and you go to live
with rock and silence." The man washes away
the blood and arranges the fish on a big plate.
Starts the onions in the hot olive oil and puts
in peppers. "You have lived all year without women."
He takes out everything and puts in the fish.
"No one knows where you are. People forget you.
You are vain and stubborn." The man slices
tomatoes and lemons. Takes out the fish
and scrambles eggs. *I am not stubborn,* he thinks,
laying all of it on the table in the courtyard
full of early sun, shadows of swallows flying
on the food. *Not stubborn, just greedy.*

The man certainly looked guilty.
Ugly, ragged, and not clean. Not to mention
their finding him there in the woods
with her body. Neighbors told how he was
always playing with dead squirrels,
mangled dogs, even snakes. He said
those were the only things that would
allow him to get close. "Look at me,"
the old man said with uncomplaining
simplicity, "I'm already one of the dead
among the dead. It's hard to watch things
humiliated the way death does it.
Possums smeared on the road, birds with ants
eating out their eyes. Even dying rats
want privacy for their disgrace.
It's true I washed the dirt from her face
and the blood off the body. Combed her hair.
I slept beside her, at her feet for two days,
the way my dog used to. I got the dress
on the best I could. She looked so neglected.
Like garbage thrown in the weeds.
Like nobody cared because he had done that
to her. I kept thinking about how long
she is going to be alone now. I knew
the police would take pictures and put them
in the papers naked and open so people
eating breakfast could look at her. I wanted
to give her spirit enough time to get ready."

THE FORGOTTEN DIALECT
OF THE HEART

How astonishing it is that language can almost mean,
and frightening that it does not quite. *Love*, we say,
God, we say, *Rome* and *Michiko*, we write, and the words
get it wrong. We say *bread* and it means according
to which nation. French has no word for home,
and we have no word for strict pleasure. A people
in northern India is dying out because their ancient
tongue has no words for endearment. I dream of lost
vocabularies that might express some of what
we no longer can. Maybe the Etruscan texts would
finally explain why the couples on their tombs
are smiling. And maybe not. When the thousands
of mysterious Sumerian tablets were translated,
they seemed to be business records. But what if they
are poems or psalms? My joy is the same as twelve
Ethiopian goats standing silent in the morning light.
O Lord, thou art slabs of salt and ingots of copper,
as grand as ripe barley lithe under the wind's labor.
Her breasts are six white oxen loaded with bolts
of long-fibered Egyptian cotton. My love is a hundred
pitchers of honey. Shiploads of thuya are what
my body wants to say to your body. Giraffes are this
desire in the dark. Perhaps the spiral Minoan script
is not a language but a map. What we feel most has
no name but amber, archers, cinnamon, horses and birds.

When I hear men boast about how passionate
they are, I think of the two cleaning ladies
at a second-story window watching a man
coming back from a party where there was
lots of free beer. He runs in and out
of buildings looking for a toilet. "My Lord,"
the tall woman says, "that fellow down there
surely does love architecture."

Barrels of chains. Sides of beef stacked in vans.
Water buffalo dragging logs of teak in the river mud
outside Mandalay. Pantocrater in the Byzantium dome.
The mammoth overhead crane bringing slabs of steel
through the dingy light and roar to the giant shear
that cuts the adamantine three-quarter-inch plates
and they flop down. The weight of the mind fractures
the girders and piers of the spirit, spilling out
the heart's melt. Incandescent ingots big as cars
trundling out of titanic mills, red slag scaling off
the brighter metal in the dark. The Monongahela River
below, night's sheen on its belly. Silence except
for the machinery clanging deeper in us. You will
love again, people say. Give it time. Me with time
running out. Day after day of the everyday.
What they call real life, made of eighth-inch gauge.
Newness strutting around as if it were significant.
Irony, neatness and rhyme pretending to be poetry.
I want to go back to that time after Michiko's death
when I cried every day among the trees. To the real.
To the magnitude of pain, of being that much alive.

VOICES INSIDE AND OUT

for Hayden Carruth

When I was a child, there was an old man with
a ruined horse who drove his wagon through the back
streets of our neighborhood, crying, *Iron! Iron!*
Meaning he would buy bedsprings and dead stoves.
Meaning for me, in the years since, the mind's steel
and the riveted girders of the soul. When I lived
on Ile Saint-Louis, a glazier came every morning,
crying *Vitre! Vitre!* Meaning the glass on his back,
but sounding like the swallows swooping years later
at evening outside my high windows in Perugia.
In my boyhood summers, Italian men came walking ahead
of the truck calling out the ripeness of their melons,
and old Jews slogged in the snow, crying, *Brooms! Brooms!*
Two hundred years ago, the London shop boys yelled
at people going by, *What do you lack?* A terrible
question to hear every day. "Less and less," I think.
The Brazilians say, "In this country we have everything
we need, except what we don't have."

We find out the heart only by dismantling what
the heart knows. By redefining the morning,
we find a morning that comes just after darkness.
We can break through marriage into marriage.
By insisting on love we spoil it, get beyond
affection and wade mouth-deep into love.
We must unlearn the constellations to see the stars.
But going back toward childhood will not help.
The village is not better than Pittsburgh.
Only Pittsburgh is more than Pittsburgh.
Rome is better than Rome in the same way the sound
of raccoon tongues licking the inside walls
of the garbage tub is more than the stir
of them in the muck of the garbage. Love is not
enough. We die and are put into the earth forever.
We should insist while there is still time. We must
eat through the wildness of her sweet body already
in our bed to reach the body within that body.

DANTE DANCING

I

When he dances of meeting Beatrice that first time,
he is a youth, his body has no real language,
and his heart understands nothing of what has
started. Love like a summer rain after drought,
like the thin cry of a red-tailed hawk, like an angel
sinking its teeth into our throat. He has only
beginner steps to tell of the sheen inside him.
The boy Dante sees her first with the absolute love
possible only when we are ignorant of each other.
Arm across his face, he runs off. Years go by.

II

The next dance is about their meeting again. He does
an *enchaînement* around her. Beatrice's heavy hair is
dark and long. She watches with the *occhi dolci*.
His jumps are a man's jumps. His steps have become
the moves of a dancer who understands the dance.
A man who recognizes the body's greed. She is deep
in her body's heart. He is splendid. She is lost
and is led away by the aunt. Her family is careful
after that. She goes by in a carriage. He rises
on his toes, *port de bras*, his eyes desperate.
Then she is at an upstairs window of the palace.
He dances his sadness brilliantly in the moonlight
below on the empty piazza, concentrating. She moves
the curtain a little to the side, and he is happy.
It is a dream we all know, the perfection of love
that is not real. There is a fountain behind him.

10

III

It is a few years later and they are finally
in his simple room. His long dance of afterward
is a declaration of joy and of gratitude and devotion.
She dances strangely, putting on her clothes.
A delicate goodbye. Her soul is free now from that
kind of love. He stands motionless, bewildered,
watching her go. Then dances his grief wonderfully.

IV

We see Dante as an old man. He is a dancer who can
manage only the simple steps of the beginning.
He dances the romance lost, the love that never was,
and the great love missed because of dreaming.
First position, *entrechat*, and the smallest jumps.
The passionate quiet. The quieter and strongest.
The special sorrow of a happy, imperfect heart
that finally knows well how to dance. But does not.

Love is apart from all things.
Desire and excitement are nothing beside it.
It is not the body that finds love.
What leads us there is the body.
What is not love provokes it.
What is not love quenches it.
Love lays hold of everything we know.
The passions which are called love
also change everything to a newness
at first. Passion is clearly the path
but does not bring us to love.
It opens the castle of our spirit
so that we might find the love which is
a mystery hidden there.
Love is one of many great fires.
Passion is a fire made of many woods,
each of which gives off its special odor
so we can know the many kinds
that are not love. Passion is the paper
and twigs that kindle the flames
but cannot sustain them. Desire perishes
because it tries to be love.
Love is eaten away by appetite.
Love does not last, but it is different
from the passions that do not last.
Love lasts by not lasting.
Isaiah said each man walks in his own fire
for his sins. Love allows us to walk
in the sweet music of our particular heart.

FINDING SOMETHING

I say moon is horses in the tempered dark,
because horse is the closest I can get to it.
I sit on the terrace of this worn villa the king's
telegrapher built on the mountain that looks down
on a blue sea and the small white ferry
that crosses slowly to the next island each noon.
Michiko is dying in the house behind me,
the long windows open so I can hear
the faint sound she will make when she wants
watermelon to suck or so I can take her
to a bucket in the corner of the high-ceilinged room
which is the best we can do for a chamber pot.
She will lean against my leg as she sits
so as not to fall over in her weakness.
How strange and fine to get so near to it.
The arches of her feet are like voices
of children calling in the grove of lemon trees,
where my heart is as helpless as crushed birds.

He keeps the valley like this with his heart.
By paying attention, being capable, remembering.
Otherwise, there would be flies as big as dogs
in the vineyard, cows made entirely of maggots,
cruelty with machinery and canvas, sniggering
among the olive trees and the sea grossly vast.
He struggles to hold it right, the eight feet
of heaven by the well with geraniums and basil.
He will rejoice even if the shepherd girl
does not pass anymore at evening. And whether
or not she ate her lamb at Easter. He knows
that loneliness is our craft, that death is
God's vigorish. He does not keep it fine
by innocence or leaving things out.

Orpheus is too old for it now. His famous voice is gone
and his career is past. No profit anymore from the songs
of love and grief. Nobody listens. Still, he goes on
secretly with his ruined alto. But not for Eurydice.
Not even for the pleasure of singing. He sings because
that is what he does. He sings about two elderly
Portuguese men in the hot Sacramento delta country.
How they show up every year or so, feeble and dressed
as well as their poverty allows. The husband is annoyed
each time by their coming to see his seventy-year-old
wife, who, long ago when they were putting through
the first railroads, was the most beautiful of all
the whores. Impatient, but saying nothing, he lets them
take her carefully upstairs to give her a bath. He does
not understand how much their doting eyes can see the sleek,
gleaming beauty of her hidden in the bright water.

Of course it was a disaster.
That unbearable, dearest secret
has always been a disaster.
The danger when we try to leave.
Going over and over afterward
what we should have done
instead of what we did.
But for those short times
we seemed to be alive. Misled,
misused, lied to and cheated,
certainly. Still, for that
little while, we visited
our possible life.

It was in the transept of the church, winter in
the stones, the dim light brightening on her,
when Linda said, Listen. Listen to this, she said.
When he put his ear against the massive door,
there were spirits singing inside. He hunted for it
afterward. In Madrid, he heard a bell begin somewhere
in the night rain. Worked his way through
the tangle of alleys, the sound deeper and more
powerful as he got closer. Short of the plaza,
it filled all of him and he turned back. No need,
he thought, to see the bell. It was not the bell
he was trying to find, but the angel lost
in our bodies. The music that thinking is.
He wanted to know what he heard, not to get closer.

The fox pushes softly, blindly through me at night,
between the liver and the stomach. Comes to the heart
and hesitates. Considers and then goes around it.
Trying to escape the mildness of our violent world.
Goes deeper, searching for what remains of Pittsburgh
in me. The rusting mills sprawled gigantically
along three rivers. The authority of them.
The gritty alleys where we played every evening were
stained pink by the inferno always surging in the sky,
as though Christ and the Father were still fashioning
the Earth. Locomotives driving through the cold rain,
lordly and bestial in their strength. Massive water
flowing morning and night throughout a city
girded with ninety bridges. Sumptuous-shouldered,
sleek-thighed, obstinate and majestic, unquenchable.
All grip and flood, mighty sucking and deep-rooted grace.
A city of brick and tired wood. Ox and sovereign spirit.
Primitive Pittsburgh. Winter month after month telling
of death. The beauty forcing us as much as harshness.
Our spirits forged in that wilderness, our minds forged
by the heart. Making together a consequence of America.
The fox watched me build my Pittsburgh again and again.
In Paris afternoons on Buttes-Chaumont. On Greek islands
with their fields of stone. In beds with women, sometimes,
amid their gentleness. Now the fox will live in our ruined
house. My tomatoes grow ripe among weeds and the sound
of water. In this happy place my serious heart has made.

MARRIED

I came back from the funeral and crawled
around the apartment, crying hard,
searching for my wife's hair.
For two months got them from the drain,
from the vacuum cleaner, under the refrigerator,
and off the clothes in the closet.
But after other Japanese women came,
there was no way to be sure which were
hers, and I stopped. A year later,
repotting Michiko's avocado, I find
a long black hair tangled in the dirt.

The rat makes her way up
the mulberry tree, the branches
getting thin and risky up close
to the fruit, and she slows.
The berry she is after is so ripe,
there is almost no red. Prospero
thinks of Christopher Smart saying
purple is black blooming. She lifts
her mouth to the berry, stretching.
The throat is an elegant gray.
A thousand shades, Christopher wrote
among the crazy people. A thousand
colors from white to silver.

The world is announced by the smell of oregano and sage
in rocky places high up, with white doves higher still
in the blue sky. Or the faint voices of women and girls
in the olive trees below, and a lustrous sea beneath that.
Like thoughts of lingerie while reading *Paradise Lost*
in Alabama. Or the boy in Pittsburgh that only summer
he was nine, prowling near the rusty railroad yard
where they put up vast tents and a man lifted anvils
with chains through his nipples. The boy listened
for the sound that made him shiver as he ran hard
across the new sawdust to see the two women again
on a platform above his head, indolent and almost naked
in the simple daylight. Reality stretched thin
as he watched their painted eyes brooding on what
they contained. He vaguely understood that it was not
their flesh that was a mystery but something on the other
side of it. Now the man remembering the boy knows
there is a door. We go through and hear a sound
like buildings burning, like the sound of a stone hitting
a stone in the dark. The heart in its plenty hammered
by rain and need, by the weight of what momentarily is.

Every morning the sad girl brings her three sheep
and two lambs laggardly to the top of the valley,
past my stone hut and onto the mountain to graze.
She turned twelve last year and it was legal
for the father to take her out of school. She knows
her life is over. The sadness makes her fine,
makes me happy. Her old red sweater makes
the whole valley ring, makes my solitude gleam.
I watch from hiding for her sake. Knowing I am
there is hard on her, but it is the focus of her days.
She always looks down or looks away as she passes
in the evening. Except sometimes when, just before
going out of sight behind the distant canebrake,
she looks quickly back. It is too far for me to see,
but there is a moment of white if she turns her face.

It should have been the family that lasted.
Should have been my sister and my peasant mother.
But it was not. They were the affection,
not the journey. It could have been my father,
but he died too soon. Gelmetti and Gregg
and Nogami lasted. It was the newness of me,
and the newness after that, and newness again.
It was the important love and the serious lust.
It was Pittsburgh that lasted. The iron and fog
and sooty brick houses. Not Aunt Mince and Pearl,
but the black-and-white winters with their girth
and geological length of cold. Streets ripped
apart by ice and emerging like wounded beasts when
the snow finally left in April. Freight trains
with their steam locomotives working at night.
Summers the size of crusades. When I was a boy,
I saw downtown a large camera standing in front
of the William Pitt Hotel or pointed at Kaufmann's
Department Store. Usually around midnight,
but the people still going by. The camera set
slow enough that cars and people left no trace.
The crowds in Rome and Tokyo and Manhattan
did not last. But the empty streets of Perugia,
my two bowls of bean soup on Kos, and Pimpaporn
Charionpanith lasted. The plain nakedness of Anna
in Denmark remains in me forever. The wet lilacs
on Highland Avenue when I was fourteen. Carrying
Michiko dead in my arms. It is not about the spirit.
The spirit dances, comes and goes. But the soul
is nailed to us like lentils and fatty bacon lodged
under the ribs. What lasted is what the soul ate.
The way a child knows the world by putting it

part by part into his mouth. As I tried to gnaw
my way into the Lord, working to put my heart
against that heart. Lying in the wheat at night,
letting the rain after all the dry months have me.

There is nothing here at the top of the valley.
Sky and morning, silence and the dry smell
of heavy sunlight on the stone everywhere.
Goats occasionally, and the sound of roosters
in the bright heat where he lives with the dead
woman and purity. Trying to see if something
comes next. Wondering whether he has stalled.
Maybe, he thinks, it is like the Noh: whenever
the script says *dances*, whatever the actor does next
is a dance. If he stands still, he is dancing.

All of it. The sane woman under the bed with the rat
that is licking off the peanut butter she puts on her
front teeth for him. The beggars of Calcutta blinding
their children while somewhere people are rich
and eating with famous friends and having running water
in their fine houses. Michiko is buried in Kamakura.
The tired farmers thresh barley all day under the feet
of donkeys amid the merciless power of the sun.
The beautiful women grow old, our hearts moderate.
All of us wane, knowing things could have been different.
When Gordon was released from the madhouse, he could
not find Hayden to say goodbye. As he left past
Hall Eight, he saw the face in a basement window,
tears running down the cheeks. And I say, nevertheless.

There is a time after what comes after
being young, and a time after that, he thinks
happily as he walks through the winter woods,
hearing in the silence a woodpecker far off.
Remembering his Chinese friend
whose brother gave her a jade ring from
the Han Dynasty when she turned eighteen.
Two weeks later, when she was hurrying up
the steps of a Hong Kong bridge, she fell,
and the thousand-year-old ring shattered
on the concrete. When she told him, stunned
and tears running down her face, he said,
"Don't cry. I'll get you something better."

To tell the truth, Storyville was brutal. The parlors
of even the fancy whorehouses crawling with roaches
and silverfish. The streets foul and the sex brawling.
But in the shabby clapboard buildings on Franklin
and on Liberty and on Iberville was the invention.
Throughout the District, you could hear Tony Jackson
and King Oliver, Morton and Bechet finding it night
after night. Like the dream Bellocq's photographs found
in the midst of Egypt Vanita and Mary Meathouse, Aunt Cora
and Gold Tooth Gussie. It takes a long time to get
the ruins right. The Japanese think it strange we paint
our old wooden houses when it takes so long to find
the *wabi* in them. They prefer the bonsai tree after
the valiant blossoming is over, the leaves fallen. When
bareness reveals a merit born in the vegetable struggling.

You hear yourself walking on the snow.
You hear the absence of the birds.
A stillness so complete, you hear
the whispering inside of you. Alone
morning after morning, and even more
at night. They say we are born alone,
to live and die alone. But they are wrong.
We get to be alone by time, by luck,
or by misadventure. When I hit the log
frozen in the woodpile to break it free,
it makes a sound of perfect inhumanity,
which goes pure all through the valley,
like a crow calling unexpectedly
at the darker end of twilight that awakens
me in the middle of a life. The black
and white of me mated with this indifferent
winter landscape. I think of the moon
coming in a little while to find the white
among these colorless pines.

There was a great tenderness to the sadness
when I would go there. She knew how much
I loved my wife and that we had no future.
We were like casualties helping each other
as we waited for the end. Now I wonder
if we understood how happy those Danish
afternoons were. Most of the time we did not talk.
Often I took care of the baby while she did
housework. Changing him and making him laugh.
I would say *Pittsburgh* softly each time before
throwing him up. Whisper *Pittsburgh* with
my mouth against the tiny ear and throw
him higher. Pittsburgh and happiness high up.
The only way to leave even the smallest trace.
So that all his life her son would feel gladness
unaccountably when anyone spoke of the ruined
city of steel in America. Each time almost
remembering something maybe important that got lost.

The monks petition to live the harder way,
in pits dug farther up the mountain,
but only the favored ones are permitted
that scraped life. The syrup-water and cakes
the abbot served me were far too sweet.
A simple misunderstanding of pleasure
because of inexperience. I pull water up
hand over hand from thirty feet of stone.
My kerosene lamp burns a mineral light.
The mind and its fierceness lives here in silence.
I dream of women and hunger in my valley
for what can be made of granite. Like the sun
hammering this earth into pomegranates
and grapes. Dryness giving way to the smell
of basil at night. Otherwise, the stone
feeds on stone, is reborn as rock,
and the heart wanes. Athena's owl calling
into the barrenness, and nothing answering.

I was carrying supplies back up the mountain
when I heard it, the laughter of children,
so strange in that starkness.
Pushed past the brush and scrub willow
and saw a ruined farmhouse and girls
in ragged clothes. They had rigged a swing
and were playing as though they were happy,
as if they did not know any better.
Having no way to measure, I thought,
remembering the man in Virginia who found
a ruined octagonal mansion
and repaired it perfectly. For months
he walked through the grand empty rooms
wondering what they were like.
Until he found a broken chair in the attic
and re-created the colors and scale. Discovered
maybe the kind of life the house was.
Strangers leave us poems to tell of those
they loved, how the heart broke, to whisper
of the religion upstairs in the dark,
sometimes in the parlor amid blazing sunlight,
and under trees with rain coming down
in August on the bare, unaccustomed bodies.

All night in the Iowa cafe. Friday night
and the farm boys with their pay.
Fine bodies and clean faces. All of them
proud to be drunk. No meanness,
just energy. At the next table, they talked
cars for hours, friends coming and going,
hollering over. The one with the heavy face
and pale hair kept talking about the Chevy
he had years ago and how it could
take everything in second.
Moaning that he should never have sold it.
Didn't he show old Hank? Bet your ass!
That Fourth of July when Shelvadeen
got too much patriotism and beer
and gave some to everybody
down by the river. Hank so mad because
I left him like he was standing still.
Best car that ever was, and never should have
let it go. Tears falling on his eggs.

I never thought Michiko would come back
after she died. But if she did, I knew
it would be as a lady in a long white dress.
It is strange that she has returned
as somebody's dalmatian. I meet
the man walking her on a leash
almost every week. He says good morning
and I stoop down to calm her. He said
once that she was never like that with
other people. Sometimes she is tethered
on their lawn when I go by. If nobody
is around, I sit on the grass. When she
finally quiets, she puts her head in my lap
and we watch each other's eyes as I whisper
in her soft ears. She cares nothing about
the mystery. She likes it best when
I touch her head and tell her small
things about my days and our friends.
That makes her happy the way it always did.

Bella fica! (beautiful fig, fine sex) the whore said
in the back streets of Livorno, proudly slapping
her groin when the man tried to get the price down.
Braddock, the heavyweight champion of the world,
when Joe Louis was destroying him, blood spraying
and his manager between rounds wanting to stop
the fight, said, I won the title in the ring,
I'm going to lose it in the ring. And, after more
damage, did. Therefore does the wind keep blowing
that holds this great Earth in the air.
For this the birds sing sometimes without purpose.
We value the soiled old theaters because of what
sometimes happens there. Berlin in the Thirties.
There were flowers all around Jesus in his agony
at Gethsemane. The Lord sees everything, and sees
that it is good despite everything. The manger
was filthy. The women at Dachau knew they were about
to be gassed when they pushed back the Nazi guard
who wanted to die with them, saying he must live.
And sang for a little while after the doors closed.

What do they say each new morning
in Heaven? They would
weary of one always
singing how green the
green trees are in
Paradise.

Surely it would seem convention
and affectation
to rejoice every time
Helen went by, since
she would have gone
daily by.

What can I say then each time
your whiteness glimmers
and fashions in the night?
If each time your voice
opens so near
in that dark

new? What can I say each morning
after that you will
believe? But there is this
stubborn provincial
singing in me,
O, each time.

PROSPERO DREAMS OF ARNAUT DANIEL
INVENTING LOVE IN THE TWELFTH CENTURY

Let's get hold of one of those deer
that live way up there in the mountains.
Lure it down with flutes, or lasso it
from helicopters, or just take it out
with a .30-30. Anyhow, we get one.
Then we reach up inside its ass and maybe
find us a little gland or something
that might make a hell of a perfume.
It's worth a try. You never know.

Not the river as fact, but the winter river,
and that river in June as two rivers.
We feel it run through our nature, the water
smelling of wet rotting just before spring,
and we call it love, a wilderness in the mind.
Mediterranean light as provender of women.
All of it contingent. This version of me
differs from another version as a vector product.
The body is a condition of the spirit.
The snow sifts down from the pines in the noon
and makes the silence even louder. A tumult
of singing when we cross the border of courtesy
into a savor of the heart. Each of us tempered
by the other, altered in ways more truly us.
We go into the secret with the shades pulled
down at dawn. Like a house on fire in sunlight.
We enable God to finally understand there is
a difference between you sitting in the clearing
confused by moonlight and you sitting in the bare
farmhouse amid the kerosene light. The two of you.

The boy came home from school and found a hundred lamps
filling the house. Lamps everywhere and all turned on
despite the summer shining in the handsome windows.
Two and three lamps on every table. Lamps in chairs
and on the rugs and even in the kitchen. More lamps
upstairs and on the topmost floor as well. All brightly
burning, until the police came and took them away.
An excess of light that continued in him for a long time.
That radiance of lamps flourishing in the day became
a benchmark for his heart, became a Beaufort scale
for his appetites. The wildness and gladness of it,
the illicitness in him magnified the careful gleam
of Paris mornings when he got to them, and the dark
glisten of the Seine each night as he crossed
the stone bridges back to his room. It was the same
years later as the snow fell through the bruised light
of a winter afternoon and he stood in a narrow street
telling Anna he was leaving. All of it a light beyond
anybody's ability to manage. The Massachusetts sunlight
lies comfortably on the maples. The Pittsburgh lamps
inside of him make it look maybe not good enough.

A YEAR LATER

for Linda Gregg

From this distance they are unimportant
standing by the sea. She is weeping, wearing
a white dress, and the marriage is almost over,
after eight years. All around is the flat
uninhabited side of the island. The water
is blue in the morning air. They did not know
this would happen when they came, just the two
of them and the silence. A purity that looked
like beauty and was too difficult for people.

On Fish Mountain, she has turned away
from the temple where they painted
pictures of Paradise everywhere inside
so that a population who prayed only
not to live could imagine yearning.
She is looking at a tree instead.
Below is a place where the man
and the beautiful woman will eat
cold noodles almost outside on a hot day.
Below that is the sound of fast water
with a barefoot woman beside it beating
an octopus on the wet stones. And then
the floor of the valley opening out onto
the yellow of blooming mustard and smoke
going straight up from large farmhouses
in the silent early evening. Where they
will walk through all of it slowly,
not talking much. A small him
and a smaller her with long black hair,
so happy together, beginning the trip
toward where she will die and leave him
looking at the back of her turned away
looking at a small tree.

"Barefoot farm girls in silk dresses," he thinks.
Meaning Marie Antoinette and the nobles
at Versailles playing at the real world.
Thinking about the elaborate seduction of ladies
and their languorous indifference in complying.
"Labored excess," he mutters, remembering
the modern Japanese calligraphers straining
at deliberate carelessness. He is still
waiting for his strange heart to moderate.
"Love as two spirits merging," he thinks,
"the flesh growing luminous and then transparent.
Who could deal with that? Like a summer lake
flickering through pine trees." It says
in Ecclesiastes that everything has its season.
A time to scatter stones and a time to gather them.
He used to wonder about the proper occasion
for casting away stones, whether it might
mean desire. He wonders if Pimpaporn went back
to her village, pictures the jungle and houses
made of teak on stilts. Tries to understand that
as a real world. Tries to know her belatedly.
He thinks of the multitude of giant rats he killed
in those cavernous, Sunday-empty, neon-dark
steel mills. Remembers piling them up on
winter nights, the weight of each, one after
the other. White mist on the black river outside.

On the beach below Spelunga everyone else is
speaking Italian, lazily paradisal in the heat.
He tries to make something of it, as though
something were going on. As though there were
something to be found in the obvious nakedness
of breasts. He complicates what is easily true,
hunting it down. It matters disproportionately
to him to see the ocean suddenly as he turns over.
He watches the afternoon as though it had
a secret. For years he will be considering
the two women nearby who decide to get lunch
at the restaurant back by the cliff. The taller
one picks up her top and tries to get
into it as they start out. But it tangles,
and she gives it indolently to the prettier one,
who puts it on as they walk away carelessly
into the garnishing Mediterranean light.

He lives in the barrens, in dying neighborhoods
and negligible countries. None with an address.
But still the Devil finds him. Kills the wife
or spoils the marriage. Publishes each place
and makes it popular, makes it better, makes it
unusable. Brings news of friends, all defeated,
most sick or sad without reasons. Shows him
photographs of the beautiful women in old movies
whose luminous faces sixteen feet tall looked out
at the boy in the dark where he grew his heart.
Brings pictures of what they look like now.
Says how lively they are, and brave despite their age.
Taking away everything. For the Devil is commissioned
to harm, to keelhaul us with loss, with knowledge
of how all things splendid are disfigured by small
and small. Yet he allows us to eat roast goat
on the mountain above Parakia. Lets us stumble
for the first time, unprepared, onto the buildings
of Palladio in moonlight. Maybe because he is not
good at his job. I believe he loves us against
his will. Because of the women and how the men
struggle to hear inside them. Because we construe
something important from trees and locomotives,
smell weeds on a hot July afternoon and are augmented.

He is shamelessly happy to feel the thing
inside him. He labors up through the pines
with firewood and goes back down again.
Winter on the way. Roses and blackberries
finished, and the iris gone before that.
The peas dead in the garden and the beans
almost done. His tomatoes are finally ripe.
The thing is inside him like that, and will
come back. An old thing, a dangerous one.
Precious to him. He meets the raccoon often
in the dark and ends up throwing stones.
The raccoon gets behind a tree. Comes again,
cautious and fierce. It stops halfway.
They stand glaring in the faint starlight.

The snow falling around the man in the naked woods
is like the ash of heaven, ash from the cool fire
of God's mother-of-pearl, moon-stately heart.
Sympathetic but not merciful. His strictness
parses us. The discomfort of living this way
without birds, among maples without leaves, makes
death and the world visible. Not the harshness,
but the way this world can be known by pushing
against it. And feeling something pushing back.
The whiteness of the winter married to this river
makes the water look black. The water actually
is the color of giant mirrors set along the marble
corridors of the spirit, the mirrors empty
of everything. The man is doing the year's accounts.
Finding the balance, trying to estimate how much
he has been translated. For it does translate him,
well or poorly. As the woods are translated
by the seasons. He is searching for a base line
of the Lord. He searches like the blind man
going forward with a hand stretched out in front.
As the truck driver ice-fishing on the big pond
tries to learn from his line what is down there.
The man attends to any signal that might announce
Jesus. He hopes for even the faintest evidence,
the presence of the Lord's least abundance. He measures
with tenderness, afraid to find a heart more classical
than ripe. Hoping for honey, for love's alembic.

MICHIKO NOGAMI (1946-1982)

Is she more apparent because she is not
anymore forever? Is her whiteness more white
because she was the color of pale honey?
A smokestack making the sky more visible.
A dead woman filling the whole world. Michiko
said, "The roses you gave me kept me awake
with the sound of their petals falling."

THE CONTAINER FOR THE
THING CONTAINED

What is the man searching for inside her blouse?
He has been with her body for seven years
and still is surprised by the arches of her
slender feet. He still traces her spine
with careful attention, feeling for the bones
of her pelvic girdle when he arrives there.
Her flesh is bright in sunlight and then not
as he leans forward and back. Picasso in his later
prints shows himself as a grotesque painter
watching closely a young Spanish woman on the bed
with her legs open and the old duenna in black
to the side. He had known nakedness every day
for sixty years. What could there be in it still
to find? But he was happy even then to get
close to the distant, distant intermittency.
Like a piano playing faintly on a second floor
in a back room. The music seems familiar, but is not.

Mogins disliked everything about Anna's pregnancy.
Said it was organs and fluids and stuff no man wanted
to know about. He was so disturbed by her milkiness
after the birth that he took his class to another part
of Denmark for the summer. When we finally made love,
the baby began to cry, and I went to get him. Anna held
the boy as we continued, until the strength went out
of her and I cradled his nakedness asleep against me
as we passed through the final stages. In the happiness
afterward, both of us nursed at her, our heads
nudging each other blindly in the brilliant dark.

THE LORD SITS WITH ME OUT IN FRONT

The Lord sits with me out in front watching
a sweet darkness begin in the fields.
We try to decide whether I am lonely.
I tell about waking at four a.m. and thinking
of what the man did to the daughter of Louise.
And there being no moon when I went outside.
He says maybe I am getting old.
That being poor is taking too much out of me.
I say I am fine. He asks for the Brahms.
We watch the sea fade. The tape finishes again
and we sit on. Unable to find words.

I wake up like a stray dog
belonging to no one.
Cold, cold, and the rain.
Friendships outgrown or ruined.
And love, dear God, the women
I have loved now only names
remembered: dead, lost, or old.
Mildness more and more the danger.
Living among rocks and weeds
to guard against wisdom.
Alone with the heart howling
and refusing to let it feed on
mere affection. Lying in the dark,
singing about the intractable
kinds of happiness.

It thrashes in the oaks and soughs in the elms,
Catches on innocence and soon dismantles that.
Sends children bewildered into life. Childhood
ends and is not buried. The young men ride out
and fall off, the horses wandering away. They get
on boats, are carried downstream, discover maidens.
They marry them without meaning to, meaning no harm,
the language beyond them. So everything ends.
Divorce gets them nowhere. They drift away from
the ruined women without noticing. See birds
high up and follow. "Out of earshot," they think,
puzzled by *earshot*. History driving them forward,
making a noise like the wind in maples, of women
in their dresses. It stings their hearts finally.
It wakes them up, baffled in the middle of their lives
on a small bare island, the sea blue and empty,
the days stretching all the way to the horizon.

Each farmer on the island conceals
his hive far up on the mountain,
knowing it will otherwise be plundered.
When they die, or can no longer make
the hard climb, the lost combs year
after year grow heavier with honey.
And the sweetness has more and more
acutely the taste of that wilderness.

Flying up, crossing over, going forward.
Passing through, getting deep enough. Breaking
into, finding the way, living at the heart
and going beyond that. Finally realizing
that arriving is not the same as being resident.
That what we do is not what we are doing.
We go into the orchard for apples. But what
we carry back is the day among trees with odor,
coolness, dappled light and time. The season
and geese going over. Always and always
with death to come, and before that the dishonor
of growing old. But meanwhile the trees are
heavy with ripe fruit. We try to visit Greece
and find ourselves instead in the pointless noon
standing among vetch and grapes, disassembling
as night climbs beautifully out of the earth
and God holds His breath. In the distance there is
the faint clatter of a farmer's bucket as she
gets water up at the well for the animals.

He stands freezing in the dark courtyard looking up
at their bright windows, as he has many nights since
moving away. Because of his promise, he does not
go up. He is thinking of the day she came back
from the hospital. They did not know her then.
He was looking down because of the happiness in her
voice talking to her husband as they went across
the courtyard. She saw him and, grinning, held up
the newborn child. Now it is the last time ever.
He finally knocks. Her eyes widen when she opens
the door. She looks to indicate her husband is home
as she unbuttons her dress. He whispers that his hands
are too cold. It will make me remember better,
she says, and puts them on her nakedness, wincing,
eyes wild with love. It is snowing when he leaves,
the narrow street lit here and there by shop windows.
Tomorrow he will be on the train with his wife, watching
the shadows on the snow. Going south to live silently
with perfect summer skies and the brilliant Aegean.

We think of lifetimes as mostly the exceptional
and sorrows. Marriage we remember as the children,
vacations, and emergencies. The uncommon parts.
But the best is often when nothing is happening.
The way a mother picks up the child almost without
noticing and carries her across Waller Street
while talking with the other woman. What if she
could keep all of that? Our lives happen between
the memorable. I have lost two thousand habitual
breakfasts with Michiko. What I miss most about
her is that commonplace I can no longer remember.

The ship goes down and everybody is lost, or is living
comfortably in Spain. He finds himself at the edge
of emptiness, absence and heat everywhere.
Just shacks along the beach and nobody in them.
He has listened to the song so often that he hears
only the spaces between the notes. He stands there,
remembering peaches. A strange, almost gray kind
that had little taste when he got them home, and that
little not much good. But there had to be a reason
why people bought them. So he decided to make jam.
When he smelled the scorching, they were already tar.
Scraped out the mess and was glad to have it over.
Found himself licking the crust on the spoon. Next day
he had eaten the rest, still not sure whether he liked
it or not. And never able to find any of them since.

MUSIC IS THE MEMORY OF WHAT NEVER HAPPENED

We stopped to eat cheese and tomatoes and bread
so good it made me foolish. The woman with me
wanted to go through the palace of the papal
captivity. Hazley and Stern said they were going
to the whorehouse. That surprised me twice
because it was only two in the afternoon.
The woman and I went to the empty palace
and met them later to drive on. They said
how neat and clean it was in the whorehouse,
and how all the men and most of the women had
been in the fourth grade together. I remember
the soft way they said it but not what they told
about going upstairs. It is not the going instead
to a blank palace where history had left no smell
that I regret. It is not even the dream
of a Mediterranean woman pulling off her dress,
the long tousled dark hair, or even the white
teeth in the shuttered room as she smiled
mischievously at the young American. I regret
the fresh coolness when they went inside from
the July heat and everybody talking quietly
as they drank ordinary wine in that promised land.

It was half a palace, half an ancient fort,
and built of mud. The home of a fierce baroness.
The rest were men, mostly elderly, and all German.
When Denise arrived, it woke them from their habits.
Not because she was exciting, since the men were
only interested in boys. But soon they were taking
turns choosing her costumes and displaying her
on low couches, or half asleep in nests of cushions
on the wonderful rugs. They did not want her naked
unless covered with jewelry. Always coaxed
her to sing, to have the awkwardness and the way
she sang off-key mix with the nipples so evident,
the heavy skirts rucked up. It dominated
the evenings. They insisted she tell stories
but did not listen to the rambling accounts
of growing up in Zurich. Two were interested
in the year she modeled for *Vogue*. More responded
to the life in Paris: fancy dinners where
perfectly dressed men and women made love to her
with hands and mouths and delicate silver instruments.
For the Germans, decadence was undistinguished,
but it mattered when they recognized the names
of nobles, the painters, and the young *couturière*
who was the sensation of that season.
What Denise remembers most from the nights
is how they ended. She and the man with her
would each choose a lad and go up to the bedroom
with the wild lamentation of the unchosen following
behind them. Most had never seen a beautiful woman.
None had seen a white one. They were desperate
in their loss. When the boys were forced out,
they pounded on the great door, a thunder searching

through the empty corridors. Some went around
to the side where her window was. Swarmed up
each other's back until there were lines up the wall
six and seven bodies high. When one reached the sill
he fell immediately, because the seeing was so intense.
A long wail and a thud, and then the whimpering
and barking began again. But what she dreams of
is the first time the Germans took her to the river.
Small figures appeared in the distance. Drifted
silently across the desert, slowly through the blur
of the heat. Soon she could see how young they were.
A few riding on horses. All discarding their clothes
as they got closer to the water. Wading, swimming
across. The black horses splashing. Stopping
in a ragged line, waiting to be chosen
for the later choosing. Mostly now she dreams
of those motionless figures in the powerful emptiness.
Wordless, shining, staring at her out of their blank faces.

He manages like somebody carrying a box
that is too heavy, first with his arms
underneath. When their strength gives out,
he moves the hands forward, hooking them
on the corners, pulling the weight against
his chest. He moves his thumbs slightly
when the fingers begin to tire, and it makes
different muscles take over. Afterward,
he carries it on his shoulder, until the blood
drains out of the arm that is stretched up
to steady the box and the arm goes numb. But now
the man can hold underneath again, so that
he can go on without ever putting the box down.

I heard a noise this morning and found two old men
leaning on the wall of my vineyard, looking out
over the fields, silent. Went back to my desk
until somebody raised the trap door of the well.
It was the one with the cane, looking down inside.
But I was annoyed when the locked door rattled where
the grain and wine were. Went to the kitchen window
and stared at him. He said something in Greek.
I spread my arms to ask what he was doing.
He explained about growing up out there long ago.
That now they were making a little walk among
the old places. Telling it with his hands.
He made a final gesture, rubbing the side
of the first finger against that of the other hand.
I think it meant how much he felt about being here
again. We smiled, even though he was half blind.
Later, my bucket banged and I saw the heavy one
pulling up water. He cleaned the mule's stone basin
carefully with his other hand. Put back a rock
for the doves to stand on and poured in fresh water.
Stayed there, touching the old letters cut in the marble.
I watched them go slowly down the lane and out
of sight. They did not look back. As I typed,
I listened for the dog at each farm to tell me
which house they went to next. But the dogs did not
bark all the way down the long bright valley.

We think the fire eats the wood.
We are wrong. The wood reaches out
to the flame. The fire licks at
what the wood harbors, and the wood
gives itself away to that intimacy,
the manner in which we and the world
meet each new day. Harm and boon
in the meetings. As heart meets what
is not heart, the way the spirit
encounters the flesh and the mouth meets
the foreignness in another mouth. We stand
looking at the ruin of our garden
in the early dark of November, hearing crows
go over while the first snow shines coldly
everywhere. Grief makes the heart
apparent as much as sudden happiness can.

He stands there baffled by pleasure and how little
it counts. The long woman is finally asleep on the bed,
the sweat beautiful on her New England nakedness.
It was while he was walking toward the shuttered window
with sunlight blazing behind it that something
important happened. He looks down through the gap
between the shutters at the Romans and late summer
in the via del Corso, trying to find a name for it,
knowing it is not love. Nor tenderness. He considers
other times just after, the random intensity sliding away,
unrecoverable. It is the sorrow that stays clear.
This specialness inside his spirit is bonded to
a knowing he cannot remember. When he was crushed,
each minor shift of his body traced out the bones
with agony, making his skeleton more and more clear
inside him. As though floodlit. He remembers
the intricate way he would lift his arm from the bed
in the hospital, turning his hand cautiously this way
and that to find the bearable paths through the air,
discovering an inch here and there where the pain
was missing. Or the cold and hunger as he walked
the alleys all night that winter down by the docks
of Genoa until each dawn, when he held the hot bowls
of tripe in his numb hands, the steam rising into his face
as he drank, the tears mixing with happiness. He opens
the shutters, and the shutters of the other window,
so the Mediterranean light can get to her. Desperately
trying to break the code while there is still time.

She told about when the American soldiers
came to the island. How the spirits would cling
to the wire fence and watch their bigness
and blondness, often without shirts, working
in the sunlight. So different from reality.
So innocent and laughing, as though it were
simple to be happy and kind. And their smell!
They had a smell that made the spirits shiver
and yearn to be material. She said that
the spirits would push long thin poles,
ivory in the moonlight, silently through
the fence, trying to touch the whiteness
those sleeping men had around their hearts.

FORAGING FOR WOOD ON THE MOUNTAIN

The wild up here is not creatures, wooded,
tangled wild. It is absence wild.
Barren, empty, stone wild. Worn-away wild.
Only the smell of weeds and hot air.
But a place where differences are clear.
Between the mind's severity and its harshness.
Between honesty and the failure of belief.
A man said no person is educated who knows
only one language, for he cannot distinguish
between his thought and the English version.
Up here he is translated to a place where it is
possible to discriminate between age and sorrow.

Once upon a time I was sitting outside the cafe
watching twilight in Umbria when a girl came
out of the bakery with the bread her mother wanted.
She did not know what to do. Already bewildered
by being thirteen and just that summer a woman,
she now had to walk past the American.
But she did fine. Went by and around the corner
with style, not noticing me. Almost perfect.
At the last instant could not resist darting a look
down at her new breasts. Often I go back
to that dip of her head when people talk
about this one or that one of the great beauties.

Night after night after hot night in the clearing.
Stars, odor of damp grass, the faint sound of waves.
The palm trees around hardly visible, and the smell
of the jungle beyond. Hour after hour of the drumming
on bells, while young girls danced elegantly in their
heavy golden costumes. Afterward, groping his way
back along the dirt paths through blackness, dazed
by the trembling music, the dancing, and their hands.
(Pittsburgh so long ago. The spoor of someone inside
him. Knowing it sometimes waiting for a train in snow,
or just a moment while eating figs in a stony field.)
One evening the rain spilled down and he ran into
the tent behind the altar, where dancers and musicians
crowded together in the unnatural light of a Coleman
lantern: the girls undressing, rain in their hair,
the delicate faces still painted, their teeth white
as they laughed. None speaking English, their language
impossible. The man finally backstage in his life.

CHASTITY

A boy sits on the porch of a wooden house,
reading *War and Peace*.
Down below, it is Sunday afternoon in August.
The street is deserted except
for the powerful sun. There is a sound,
and he looks. At the bottom of the long
flight of steps, a man has fallen.
The boy gets up, not wanting to.
All year he has thought about honesty,
and he sits down. Two people finally come
and call the ambulance.
But too late. When everybody is gone,
he reads some pages, and stops.
Sits a moment, turns back to the place,
and starts again.

The sultry first night of July, he on the bed
reading one of Chandler's lesser novels.
What he should be doing is in the other room.
Today he began carrying wood up from the valley,
already starting on winter. He closes the book
and goes naked into the pitch pines and the last
half-hour of the dark. Rain makes a sound
on the birches and a butternut tree. There is not
enough time left to use it for dissatisfaction.
Often it is hard to know when the middle game
is over and the end game beginning, the pure part
that is made more of craft than it is of magic.

Maybe when something stops, something lost in us
can be heard, like the young woman's voice that
seemed to come from an upstairs screened porch.
There were no lights in the house, nor in the other
houses, at almost one o'clock. The muffled sweet
moans changed as she changed from what she was not
into the more she was. The small panting became
the gasping. Never getting loud but growing
ever more evident in the leafy summer street.
Whimpers and keening, a perishing, then nothing.
In the silence, the man outside began to unravel,
maybe altering. Maybe altering more than that.

I imagine the gods saying, We will
make it up to you. We will give you
three wishes, they say. Let me see
the squirrels again, I tell them.
Let me eat some of the great hog
stuffed and roasted on its giant spit
and put out, steaming, into the winter
of my neighborhood when I was usually
too broke to afford even the hundred grams
I ate so happily walking up the cobbles,
past the Street of the Moon
and the Street of the Birdcage-Makers,
the Street of Silence and the Street
of the Little Pissing. We can give you
wisdom, they say in their rich voices.
Let me go at last to Hugette, I say,
the Algerian student with her huge eyes
who timidly invited me to her room
when I was too young and bewildered
that first year in Paris.
Let me at least fail at my life.
Think, they say patiently, we could
make you famous again. Let me fall
in love one last time, I beg them.
Teach me mortality, frighten me
into the present. Help me to find
the heft of these days. That the nights
will be full enough and my heart feral.

Gradually he could hear her. Stop, she was saying,
stop! And found the bed full of glass,
his ankles bleeding, driven through the window
of her cupola. California summer. That was pleasure.
He knows about that: stained glass of the body
lit by our lovely chemistry and neural ghost.
Pleasure as fruit and pleasure as ambush. Excitement
a wind so powerful, we cannot find a shape for it,
so our apparatus cannot hold on to the brilliant
pleasure for long. Enjoyment is different.
It understands and keeps. The having of the having.
But ecstasy is a question. Doubling sensation
is merely arithmetic. If ecstasy means we are
taken over by something, we become an occupied
country, the audience to an intensity we are
only the proscenium for. The man does not want
to know rapture by standing outside himself.
He wants to know delight as the native land he is.

Light is too bare, too simple for her. She has lived
in the darkness so long, she prefers it. Sits among
the shrubs in the woods at night, singing of Orpheus,
who sings prettily but innocently. She knows we are
rendered by time, by pain and desire, so makes a home
always in the present. He still dotes on what was lost
and the losing of it, his cracked voice singing of his
young voice singing about love. The dark has derived
an excitement from her. Eurydice sings of passion
as a foreign country. Says candles made from birds
and tigers, from tallow of fox and snake, burn with
a troubling radiance. Orpheus sings about the smell
of basil growing in the rusting five-gallon can
on the wall between his vineyard and the well.
Eurydice tells of animals searching each other
on the bed meanwhile, shameful and vibrant.
He sings of soup cooking in the dented pot.
Of how fine it was out there in the stony fields,
eating and grieving and solitary year after year.

Sixteen years old, surrounded by beasts in the pens
at two in the morning. The animals invisible.
Clumsy sounds of their restlessness in the dark.
Touching them. Not for the risk, but for the clues.
Not for the danger. Searching into the difference,
and the smell of wildness all around. The stink
of yaks and hyenas, the wet breathing of buffalo.
There is no handbook, no map for his heart in there,
no atlas for his spirit ever. The only geography
we have is the storybooks of our childhood. We go
step by step, mouthful and handful at a time.
Is this an apple? Yes, it tastes like an apple.
The bible says the good place is somewhere else.
This somewhere else is certainly not that one.
He had no hope of getting to what he seemed to be.
When I think of him among camels, tapirs, and llamas,
it reminds me of the banquets of Japanese emperors.
Each dish of marvelous food was put in front of
the guest and, after a while, taken away untouched.
Course after course. I remember that youth I was
and wonder if it is the same way with the soul.
They never learned whether the emperor's food was
just much better or if it was something beyond that.
We end up asking what our lives really tasted like.

I found another baby scorpion today. Tiny,
exquisite, and this time without his mother.
Alone in a bag of onions. I wonder
what was between them, this mother and babe.
Does she grieve now someplace up there hanging
by her claws as she makes her way awkwardly
back and forth across my bamboo ceiling?
Is there a bewildered sound? Like the goat
calling her eaten kid for three long days.
Is there a thin, whispery voice I can't hear
going back and forth? Which the Chinese elm
hears. Which the grapes and ants, the spiders
and the rat I won't let in hear. Or is it insectal?
The sound of apparatus? Did she feed him incidentally
beside her? Did they sleep unafraid? Merely alert?
Not needing to touch the other first?

How could he later on believe it was the best
time when his wife died unexpectedly
and he wandered every day among the trees, crying
for more than a year? He is still alone and poor
on the island with wild flowers waist-deep
around his stone hut. In June the wind will
praise the barley stretching all the way
to the mountain. Then it will be good
in the harvested fields, with the sun nailed
to the stony earth. Mornings will come and go
in the silence, the moon a heaven mediated
by owls in the dark. Is there a happiness
later on that is neither fierce nor reasonable?
A time when the heart is fresh again, and a time
after that when the heart is ripe? The Aegean
was blue just then at the end of the valley,
and is blue now differently.

All that remains from the work of Skopas
are the feet. Sometimes not even that.
Sometimes only irregularities on the plinth
that may indicate how the figure stood.
Using the feet, or shadows of feet,
and the exact diagrams of German professors,
learned men argue about what the arms
were doing and how good the sculpture was.
As we do with our lives, guessing whether
the woman was truly happy when it rained
and if her father was really the ambassador.
Whether she was passionate or just wanted to please.

They dragged me down. Down the muddy hill
with me frantically digging in my heels,
grabbing at bushes and weeds. Kicking
and bellowing, I was pulled down and under
the bridge. Dead for sure, I thought,
now that I was out of sight. They had me on
my back and were stomping, driving in
their heavy shoes and hurting me
with their fists. Me yelling no! no! no!
and twisting away, furious. And them,
furious, trying to kill me now because
I was too dumb to give in. Afterward,
sitting at the bus stop cleaning off
the blood, something in me wanted to know
what I was like in the middle of it,
down there under the bridge.

The woman is asleep in the bedroom. The fan is making
its sound and the television is on behind him
with the sound off. The chuck-will's-widow is calling
in the scrub across the asphalt road. Farther on,
the people are asleep in their one-story houses
with the lawn outside and the boat in the driveway.
He is thinking of the British Museum. These children
drive fast when they are awake. Twenty years ago
this was a swamp with alligators and no shape.
He is thinking of the Danish cold that forced him
into the gypsy girl's bed. Like walking through
a door and finding Venezia when he thought he was
in Yugoslavia. The people here seem hardly here
at all: blond desire always in the middle of
air conditioning. He remembers love as it could be.
Outside, the moon is shining on nothing in particular.

The air this morning is pleasant and praises nothing.
It lies easily on each thing. The light has no agency.
In this kind of world, we are on our own: the plain
black shoes of a man sitting in the doorway,
pleats of the tall woman's blue skirt as she hurries
to an office farther on. We will notice maybe
the gold-leaf edges of a book carried by the student
glinting intermittently as she crosses into the bright
sunlight on our side of the street. But usually
we depend on meditation and having things augmented.
We see the trees in their early-spring greenness,
but not again until just before winter. The common
is mostly beyond us. Love after the fervor, the wife
after three thousand nights. It is easy to realize
the horses suddenly running through an empty alley.
But marriage is clear. Like the faint sound of a cello
very late at night somewhere below in the stillness
of an old building on a street named Gernesgade.

I light the lamp and look at my watch.
Four-thirty. Tap out my shoes
because of the scorpions, and go out
into the field. Such a sweet night.
No moon, but urgent stars. Go back inside
and make hot chocolate on my butane burner.
I search around with the radio through
the skirl of the Levant. "Tea for Two"
in German. Finally, Cleveland playing
the Rams in the rain. It makes me feel
acutely here and everybody somewhere else.

Do you think it's easy for him, the poor bastard?
To be that weak whenever their music begins?
It's not a convenient delight, not a tempered scale.
Not a choice. As Saint Francis had no choice,
needing to be walled up in his stone cell all winter.
To be flogged through Assisi naked and foul.
God is not optional when faith is like that.
But Francis had a vocation, not a need for silly women.
Giovanni really believes they are important.
Talks about them as parallel systems. Crazy stuff.
An educated gentleman of the finest family
wandering off helplessly after their faintest glimmer.
He believes there is a secret melded with the ladies.
He smiles and nods all evening as he listens
to their chatter and the whining about their husbands.
He says the world changes because of them.
Their flesh unfolds and he goes through to something
beyond the flesh. Hears a voice, he says.
A primitive radio at the core of them.
Growing and fading, as though it comes from the moon.

I had not seen her for twenty years when she called
to welcome me back to America, wanting to see me.
Warning that she was past forty now and the mother
of a seven-year-old. The lost time flooded me.
Paris and me without money or a place to take her.
I borrowed a room and lit candles and had wine.
It went badly. My knees kept sliding away under me
on the starched sheets. I managed the humiliation
by turning my back and refusing to talk. She was
as young as I was and felt, I suspect, relief.

The birds do not sing in these mornings. The skies
are white all day. The Canadian geese fly over
high up in the moonlight with the lonely sound
of their discontent. Going south. Now the rains
and soon the snow. The black trees are leafless,
the flowers gone. Only cabbages are left
in the bedraggled garden. Truth becomes visible,
the architecture of the soul begins to show through.
God has put off his panoply and is at home with us.
We are returned to what lay beneath the beauty.
We have resumed our lives. There is no hurry now.
We make love without rushing and find ourselves
afterward with someone we know well. Time to be
what we are getting ready to be next. This loving,
this relishing, our gladness, this being puts down
roots and comes back again year after year.

RESPECT

for Albert Schweitzer

This morning I found a baby scorpion,
perfect, in the saucepan.
Killed it with a piece of marble.

Trying to scrape the burned soup from my only pan
with a spoon after midnight by oil lamp
because if I do not cook the mackerel
this hot night it will kill me tomorrow
in the vegetable stew. Which is twice
wasteful. Though it would be another way
of cutting down, I am thinking, as I go out to get
more water from the well and happen to look up
through the bright stars. Yes, yes, I say,
and go on pulling at the long rope.

The soft wind comes sweet in the night
on the mountain. Invisible except for
the sound it makes in the big poplars outside
and the feel on his naked, single body,
which breathes quietly a little before dawn,
eyes open and in love with the table
and chair in the transparent dark and stars
in the other window. Soon it will be time
for the first tea and cool pear and then
the miles down and miles up the mountain.
"Old and alone," he thinks, smiling.
Full of what abundance has done to his spirit.
Feeling around inside to see if his heart
is still, thank God, ambitious. The way
old men look in their eyes each morning.
Knowing she isn't there and how much Michiko
isn't anywhere. The eyes close as he remembers
seeing the big owl on the roof last night
for the first time after hearing it for months.
Thinking how much he has grown unsuited
for love the size it is for him. "But maybe
not," he says. And the eyes open as he
grins at the heart's stubborn pretending.

She lives, the bird says, and means nothing
silly. She is dead and available,
the fox says, knowing about the spirits.
Not the picture at the funeral,
not the object of grieving. She is dead
and you can have that, he says. If you can
love without politeness or delicacy,
the fox says, love her with your wolf heart.
As the dead are to be desired.
Not the way long marriages are,
nothing happening again and again.
Not in the woods or in the fields.
Not in the cities. The painful love of being
permanently unhoused. Not color, but the stain.

The goldfish is dead this morning on the bottom
of her world. The autumn sky is white,
the trees are coming apart in the cold rain.
Loneliness gets closer and closer.
He drinks hot tea and sings off-key:
This train ain't a going-home train, this train.
This is not a going-home train, this train.
This train ain't a going-home train 'cause
my home's on a gone-away train. That train.

ACKNOWLEDGMENTS

Jack Gilbert wishes to acknowledge the following publishers of
the poems included in this volume:

American Poetry Review: "Tear It Down," "To See If Something
Comes Next," "Betrothed," "Adulterated," "The White Heart of
God," "Man at a Window"

Columbia: "Prospero Dreams of Arnaut Daniel Inventing Love
in the Twelfth Century"

Harcourt Brace & Co.: "The Lord Sits with Me Out in Front,"
"Foraging for Wood on the Mountain," "The Lives of Famous
Men" (in *Nineteen Poets of the Golden Gate*, 1984)

The Iowa Review: "A Year Later," "Gift Horses," "Ghosts," "In
Umbria," "Leporello on Don Giovanni," "Almost Happy"

Ironwood: "Prospero Without His Magic," "Haunted
Importantly"

The Nation: "Playing House"

New Letters: "Hard Wired," "Harm and Boon in the Meetings,"
"I Imagine the Gods," "Thinking about Ecstasy," "How to Love
the Dead"

Ploughshares: "Voices Inside and Out"

Poetry: "What Is There to Say?"

Poetry East: "Searching for Pittsburgh," "Steel Guitars," "Tasters
for the Lord"

The Quarterly: "Going Wrong," "1953," "Looking Away from
Longing," "Theoretical Lives" (as "Everybody Knew but Gave
Different Answers")

Virginia Quarterly: "Older Women," "Music Is the Memory of
What Never Happened," "Michiko Dead"

JACK GILBERT was born in Pittsburgh. He is the author of *Refusing Heaven; Monolithos*, which was a finalist for the Pulitzer Prize; and *Views of Jeopardy*, the 1962 winner of the Yale Younger Poets Prize. He has also published a limited edition of elegaic poems under the title *Kochan*. A recipient of a Guggenheim Fellowship and a grant from the National Endowment for the Arts, Gilbert lives in Northampton, Massachusetts.